THEM GONE

THEM GONE

Akua Lezli Hope

THE WORD WORKS
WASHINGTON D.C.

The Word Works
P.O. Box 42164
Washington, D.C. 20015
editor@wordworksbooks.org

Cover art: El Anatsui, "Akua's Surviving Children," 1996.
Found wood and metal, dimensions variable.
Image courtesy of October Gallery.
Author photograph: Brad Turner
Cover design: Susan Pearce

LCCN: 2018931398
ISBN: 978-1-944585-25-9

The cross-out passages in "Soufrière Speaks" are derived from the website page of the Montserrat Volcano Observatory, and the Weekly Volcanic Report, a cooperative project between the Smithsonian's Global Volcanism Program and the US Geological Survey's Volcano Hazards Program, and the *Washington Post*.

The epigraph for "Our Cousin's Children" is from Stanton Peele's website www.peele.net, © 1996-2016. "FAQ Crack Babies."

Acknowledgments

My everlasting gratitude to these publications for including my words:
   African American Review: "Hairdressers"
   ARTSCOPE: "She knits acrylic hosannas..."
   Contact/II, a Poetry Review: "For Bob Thompson"
   Hambone: "Afro Funk"
   Stone Canoe: "Seneca"
   Ordinary Women: "my mother is an indictment ...",
   Obsidian II, Black Literature in Review: "950 Hoe Avenue,"
     "Acknowledgment," "Village You Come From"
   What Is Found There: Notebooks on Poetry and Politics:
     "To Every Birth Its Pain"
   Three Coyotes: "Plant"

And thanks to the following anthologies for including these poems:
   *My Soul to His Spirit: Soulful Expressions from Black Daughters to
     Their Fathers*: "Dancing on Daddy's Feet"
   Cave Canem Anthology: "The Them Gone"
   The Year's Best Writing, Writer's Digest Guides: "Hard Won
     Country"
   Words of Wisdom: Poet's Theater 20th Anniversary Anthology:
     "My Mommy Gone #15"

Thank you to the New York Foundation for the Arts, The National Endowment for the Arts, and The Ragdale Foundation for the grants that affirmed, strengthened, enabled.

Thank you to all those who rescued me from starvation and destitution when I became paralyzed, including Andrea Bempong, Anton Bestebreurtje, Judy Serkin, Karen and Jim Alpha, Lois Welk, Miriam Hardin Hunter, Marilyn McMillan, Noeva Wong, Jacqueline Johnson, Carolyn Micklem; to my neighbors, Connie and Louise Sullivan-Blum for saving my home, and to all the other poets and creators who contributed their energy and resources to my salvation and restoration. I am so grateful for your efforts on my behalf.

Thank you to Nancy White for her kindness and rigor, and to The Word Works for choosing *Them Gone* and making it manifest.

Thank you to Cave Canem for hope, connection, and community: I am because we are.

Contents

I

950 Hoe Avenue

(The Bronx)

The child does not love this place
      It is skin   it is light   it is
      her bubble bath
      her curtains lifting
      her yellow records on
      her record player
          let us give three cheers for Gaston and Josephine
          i'll be a sunbeam for Jesus
      her stack of golden books
      her room next to her parents
      the long list for God to bless each night
      her forbidden short cut through the alley to school
      her treasured malteds at the fountain with Daddy
            with an egg for health
      and special sundaes on the boulevard with Mommy
      she loves them but not this place
      this five flights up
      these French doors
      this first to conquer living space
      Castro sofa pull-out bed
      where nights of blue glow heaven she waits
      with Mommy, watching old myths,
      Flynn, Fontaine, Niven, De Haviland, for Daddy
      She does not love the fire escape
      where she can glimpse other peoples' lives
      where summer brings *baratata* musics
      (where her parents heard John Cage's 777 misplayed
      and Makeba's clicks and trills shaped that age)
      nor does she love her friends
      black, blonde, brown, beige
      where she met yogurt, hammen-
      taschen, tortillas, grits
      it took forever to learn to fight, fit, roller skate
      concrete claimed her knees
      she has blooded this place.
      for her there was no before,
      she has not come to after
      she does not hold these memories –
      the adult she becomes summons the ghosts,
      holds the after,
      loves that nonexistent place.

Our Cousins' Children

The original alarmist projections that crack babies were permanently damaged proved unfounded. Dr. Ira Chasnoff found that their "average developmental functioning level is normal." Dr. Claire likewise re-evaluated her initial assessments of these children, and decided the worst damage these infants experienced seemed to occur in their worlds after birth. — Stanton Peele

I

> *It's funny,*
> *they don't remember*
> *their mother's face*
> > *6 months gone;*
> *but they remember being*
> *tied to a bed*
> > *eating dog food*
> *they remember needles*

They remember hunger,
quick shifts in mood
your sudden laughter is another gunshot
> *these children – 5, 4, 2, and 8 months*
> *are ready to survive*
you must bring blankets
though touch is thorn as much as rose

place a buoy
though their flailing furies resist assistance
don't want them to drown

learn to navigate without license
follow lines to their scary source
> *they cannot use adults for solace*
untangle knots you never knew existed

not wise   used beyond their years
not only a child looks out from their eyes

II

Every parting requires preparation
must be there
when she comes home from school
no subs   no fill-ins   no backstops

be there all night
as he sleepwalks to be sure
leave the light on
in the bedroom and the hall

III

At five, Johnnie knew how to read and count
because his own hunger needed feeding,
he shopped for the household, was her little man

Desiree had not let him be dropped out some window
she leapt for his life

then left it:

cleaned up with methadone
first day home, hit a C too high, too pure,
too much, with old friends

her sister, Saint Donna, had asked for him before
got him then, to be her second son
and with her husband Larry, try to raise whole men

toilet trained at nine months, bed wetting at nine
when nightmares return to police his sleep
is he loved enough to keep getting clean sheets?

he didn't cry 'til he was nineteen

Hard Won Country

She drives him to school
through this hard-won rural suburbia
where the only visible thorns
adorn scant thistle and rosebushes
reaching spring branches through chain link fences.
No yellow bus for him, no MTA,
he will be safely ferried to learn and play.
The shouts that rocked the bus she rode
where the quick northern mob gathered
to torment her elementary
way home from gifted classes,
will never reach his ears.
He'll never have to dodge the sudden legs
or feet in dirty, narrow aisles as he makes his way
to the once pre-designated rear
neither will he hear those low,
ancient moans from stench-drenched vessels,
lynchtree and jailhouse groans,
nor their reverberating why.
She will stand guard
against even her fear, memory, pain,
use bleach every Saturday,
dust, vacuum, sponsor play dates,
host thrill-packed birthday parties,
drive the Jeep made for snow, rain,
and this ever-changing terrain.
Each day convey her son
to school, soccer, safety, success.

New David

for David Max Coltrane Dylan Geemun Wong Chong

Move to the womb's remembered rhythm.
Your mother sings what she knows
jackson browne, no light lullabies
maybe later. when you learn the right
breast as easily as you seek the left, where
her heart sings the beat that grew you.

Whatever we need, however we grow you,
you're soon on your own. Remember that rhythm,
remember that heart is your home – the where
that you'll live. The one thing that knows
teach it some truth - or what seems right
Baby, you need kinder lullabies.

Not loneliness of long distance runners, lullabies
all this muck too soon. A sweet arc of sounds for you
Blow some blues, some jazz, to get it right
hand drums, cymbals, some junggwo city rhythm.
Geemun, your mother sings what she knows,
your ears hold another future, another where.

Remember your heart is your home, the where
and how you'll live. All these unremembered lullabies
we give you. Fractured hymns humming who knows
which effort clicks, which hug shapes you
as certain as her heartbeat, your first rhythm.
Add some chants, Chinatown's polyphonies, please get it right.

Maybe later. when you'll learn the right
breast as quickly as you suck the left where
you move toward womb's remembered rhythm
You'll graduate to those perverse lullabies
your mother sings to give you all she knows
her life changes and she learns to grow you

You are too new to know this. Need fuels you.
Born of cruelest month, comfort is still your right
the world's denials await. We hope you'll never know
tiny scholar. You will work, play, own anywhere
We sing you open, sing you strong, fierce lullabies
you've inherited a manifest of rhythm.

Just learn the right side. Incoherent lullabies
are all comfort songs from everywhere. Know
this world's rhythms, know your heart; home is you.

Building History Lullaby

You are the history we build.
You won't remember this –
I came to see your first play:

You are the narrator
your proud mother invited me
and we bear witness to your triumph.
O lone black boy, I clap and clap and clap
and take pictures and praise you excessively
for your part in the Three Piggy Opera

Such is my joy to do again the unremembered
thing you will most forget.
My siblings don't remember stories I read them,
nor our tea parties, but their children are read to
and play elaborate pretends

To give you the gift we had
of so much love that you don't have to remember
you won't have to remember:
someone will always be there
others will always know and ask for you
someone will always care,
it will be a link, a chain, a plate in your invisible armor
to arise and wrap you in the forcefield
of our hope for you and your promise.

Village You Come From

The reach, the rush   in the rush of the jets
the wish, the whoosh in our ears
the screech, the roar, the run of low sky
the crash, the hush in comingclose night

We shut the screens
We stood in backyards
We raised our palms to our eyes

We watched through tall grass
We leaned on the car
We ate the barbequed dogs

We scanned the haze
We pulled the clothesline
We bicycled over to see

Where wings ran loud
rang thunder, wrenched pride
that village you come from in Queens.

Seneca

The first time your visiting nephew
rode Captain Bill's narrative boat
he was afraid. Though the dark
polished wood interior, solid,
brown, comforting with flowered
seat cushions, was bright as a Sunday parlor,
sunshine on boat's wake made waves
teeth and knives. You know how
to swim, yellow orange candy-colored
lifesavers overhead. Nothing bad
will happen to you, but it already had.
Skinny adolescent narrator pauses, captain details
where those before walked. Assiniki, stony place
of people whose path is that faint narrow rock ledge
descending, disappearing into gray shattering shore wall
Salt mines across this deepest Finger Lake
another mysterious steaming of stuff from below.
All this strangeness and feeling yourself
a small, small thing on a big indifference.

Being Here

De Kock's father beat him,
was an alcoholic, though his
murderous son says "big, strong, strict."
We see how a stick was bent to life-snuffing sick,
stuck in a culture blinded to its colonial perdition.

In democratic purgatory,
I work to see monsters as human,
that next-door neighbor threatening harm
just an ill-bred girl.
I save money for expensive fences,
cast sea salt along the narrow border.

I pray, moments before a class of fledgling raptors
and grendahls, that my transitory presence makes them rethink
the drone of hate and fear they return to each afternoon,

that by showing them their power to create,
boys won't make mine an automatic target,
girls might write their way to strength,

and not repeat their mothers
and not make more evil sons.

*De Kock was the South African official who kidnapped,
tortured, and murdered many anti-apartheid ativists.*

II

I Will Not Run into Ted

I will not run into Ted in Paris
after leaving a message that Odile can no longer take at the Village
Voice, which no longer exists, and no café crème upstairs and their
falling out or whatever it ever was and the change of management and
style it is gone gone gone

I will not run into Ted because I posted a message at Shakespeare
where they will tell me he hasn't been in 4 months and they are
annoyed by the pile of mail but come come upstairs and see some
secrets, see this cushy place where words spiraled to heaven and back
like a umbilicus, like a bean stalk, like a spiral ladder, where Joyce
joyced and Stein steined and Ted teducated

I will not run into Ted wearing the pin of winged lips which I must
make again, which he wanted as it was the time of wearing pins like
medals of art accomplishment not war, lipwings

I will not wing into Ted at the Musée National des Arts d'Afrique et
d'Océanie above the crocodiles and near the best stolen African Art
across from the rowboat pond adjacent the zoo

I will not run into Ted there at the celebration of young African poets
declaiming in enunciated French so that even I could understand, pride and
urgency filling this auditorium of new age colonizers, how it still mattered

I will not run onto Ted running with my new husband who is no
longer new and no longer my husband running for a gateau to take to
Ted's apartment to see a Teducationfilm, as his test was to meet the
gift of the occasion with whatever you could muster to share, as I had
learned in past run-ins

I will not run into Ted talking about that bama of a goofy girl who was
crashing his pad and spoiling his mack on the Asian dancer, "imagine
the children," he whispered

I will not run into Ted again with Ed Clarke who was making
monumental clouds in the city of artists and the delicious Ethiopian
princess they nibbled with their eyes who was beautiful though badly
behaved who never brought a cake or bought a café

I will not run into Ted above the Seine on the best bridge in Paris

I will not run into Ted on the top of Samaritaine, showing me the best
free view of Paris

I will not run into Ted as a dream I dreamt in college and a dream I
met and shared with Dusty and Barry who won the Watson meeting
him awake dreaming and carried news of how I wanted to run into him

I will not run into Ted in Timbucktu or Tomboucktou in mythic
museums of mystery where Billie and Bessie sang with the Dogon

I will not run into Ted painting *Bird Lives!* on dawn streets of
indifference transmuting negro feet to black wings

I will not run into Ted with his Valkyrie glugging brew from a stein
in a café where everyone else sipped

I will not run into Ted demystifying Ella's "How High the Moon"
and enshrining Langston Hughes

I will not run into Ted telling me the secret phone number for the
weekly Parisian potluck where the Polish actress spoke of border
crossings and armed interrogations and the landshaper spoke of
reformation and terraforming and the eating was scrumptious

I will not run into Ted rewarding my diligence, for going to weird
places and getting black postcards for his collection 20 years before
acquisitive hoards valued them

I will not run into Ted hearing a new thing, Ornette's double
bending multiplied sound growing roots from magma, an earth
spout umbilicus, spiraling upward

I will not run into Ted in the Village for the moment, in town for
a couple of days, striding sauntering past Café Reggio saying hi with
cool surprise, I can hear his voice. yes, yes, I can hear his voice a last bit
of groove at record's end but you do not know ghosts in vinyl except
through scratching so you will not run into Ted

I will not run into Ted looking gleamingly glorious grey and bronze,
dimple-lined on the cover of the oversized Paris magazine, hip dean
of black ex-pats I never saw and when I saw some they didn't speak, but
Ted would speak,

Ted spoke, pierced pufferies and joked
and shared and laughed and taught and

I will not run into Ted anymore.

*For Ted Joans (1928 – 2003), an American jazz
poet, surrealist, trumpeter, painter and friend.*

Evocateur

for Eartha Kitt

Your purr was always there
How catwoman, a role you made your own
was inhabited as shape shifter transmutes flesh
making us believe along
that this human is something else
and more

your fluidity sprung from
being beaten
metal made malleable early
after your forging in rough nameless times
unfathered streets and pass along mothers
poorly shod feet and indifferent others
What did Orson Welles taste in your blood

in your bitten lip?
holding you close was not enough
kissing did not teach
his hungry genius yearned to know your secret
only in some bloodletting
might he glimpse the mystery
of your transformative magics

Not just the must of recreation, lemons into aid
where is sugar?
where is water?
there was only this blood still wanting
with a community of riches
but no family to focus your light
How some light must blaze brighter
to not be extinguished
nameless times of foodlessness,
ragged, bare, singular in want when you can see
through windows of great stores of promise

When along wide Harlem boulevards
that concrete Mecca, Black folk did promenade,
hatted, coiffed, well shod
as from cabarets, clubs, bars,
distant tinkles of laughter, joy, music
suggest you take this in and envision
yourself fabled, fabulous
so you carve your talent

with movement, with work
with your own fanned flame
your own coals carried in singed heart
Now your name is known, held dear
Eartha, as your voice held us
curled us around you
spun us up, your erotic ferocity
velvet whips, your recitative trill
cajoled, commanded, electric
to watch as you simmered or blazed in every camera angle
whenever you were there, you, we watched
and then these late, later years
teaching dance, passing your body's gift on
your effort to give, transfuse
as all great ones do
shamans loving us into better selves
dancing us, singing us anew

For Bob Thompson

Because you burnt
Because you imploded
Because you mortared angels with pigment
Because you flirted with redemption
          and felt her sister, notoriety's ass
Because you fingered the snatch of death and licked your index
Because a man I loved wanted you and a white angel more than me
Because you were a junejazzer, a homeboy hanging out with a slick crew
          – archie and the short jones
Because you mashed the monsters and prayed
Because you deconstructed eurofigures on a newworld plane
          and colored changes
Because we are all expelled and blurred and joined
          even if we won't believe
Because of shadow
Because you were the bird

Bob Thompson was a prolific, though short-lived, African American artist who produced over 1,000 works in his eight-year career. His work employed singular cultural referents and evocative symbols.

Afro Funk

Some say it's the corolla of Afro
on velvet canvas goddesses
implacable on village sidewalks
near Bboys from Corona
watching pickup ball near the maw of subway

Others say nah, it's ineffable, like
the young brothers' lean in they walk
sisters' swish in they leather wrapped
booties the rootie tootie of swayback
the bend of fantasy at bowlegs
where muscle rounds the curve.
who first wore layers
staccato art-furrowed heads
whose kente woven scarf
meets momma's best made

When every sunday dinner is a feast
or summer barbeque in backyard queens
means miles of pungent flesh
grilled in ritual offering, smokes.
and the combat of rival stereos
floats through the haze...
as the thump and blaze of need-to-bes
rise from half-finished basements

is that it?

No One Comes Home to Lonely Women

she runs coatless
colder than winter
no metaphor for why.
burning metaphors must keep her warm
behind the wild whorl she uses as eyes
it is Riviera with the Italian dude
she bragged, maddened by her dark
wine and pixie face
bagged by close ensnaring wind of her hair,
scent of dusky kush cotton
romans always wuz collectors

or maybe it's spring wid her black collegiate
his big thing and campus women
green-eyein, dyin for her to go back home
was it bad men?

could be summer again
teachin art to project kids
slidin to home plate through wine bottle
salaried enough to keep tryin
dumb enough to care.
where we met, she was Black Phoebe
near peer, lark ascending
was it frustration?

madness did not steal her youth:
under a sullen rusty wig
a pixie glimmer haunts her face
Pat, is that you, head in washing machine
enclosed in remote glee of some unheard joke
God does protect fools: not one
panty nor suds fell out machine's mindless whirl

she slow straightened (the other pushed aside)
assumed a still remembered attitude of spine, shoulder
and eye flashed recognition and spoke
bourgie chitchat lingo

why didn't i grab you
slap or hold you
could no one love you?

i didn't know her well enough to cry
but knew enough to wonder why
how she be like SRO men
state's waste howling
on slush streetcorners
at noon high and mid/night

She sails down Broadway
defiance in her chestchin thrust
mute compliance in bare, crossed arms

reach for just bought coffee
look for a five – can't spare a dime
i run slow-mo   heavy boots
three-pair socks   two sweaters
ten ton coat...

and like Billie Bessie Zora

she is gone.

Even Though

Even though you have religion
you worship with me: words in words
this world to save
my Jesus body is broken
an unrisen cripple rolls toward you
hoping to wield smart weapons
heal the inattention to essentials,
reality. I too craved cunning purses
to carry petty esthetics of fashion's fleeting moment
ignored burdens to be born, to be laid down
or left as tips in diners, spent petals scattered
on petroleum-shining seas
I too drank wild rivers, fractured sensory meaning
into chemical transcendences
Blooming trees in Bronx, Harlem, Brooklyn
wherever concrete cracked
Bent by loss, smacked by grief upon too-soon-gone grief
legion of my superheroes thinned
to we few, bent shoulder to shoulder
murmuring prayers and half-remembered
incantations, tracing songlines through steel canyons
huddled around an ashcan
fire roasting yams against the cold
feed our dreaming multitude.

Kwansaba

for Jayne Cortez

Acid tongue, lash putrid meme from thought
Atomic coppice, bloom laser snakes, whip frenzy
Writhe Hendrick's helix licks, soar Bessie's dare
Outplay sound crushers, arrest water thieves, redeem
betrayed futures from oil-slicked bloody seas
Seize us epileptic seer, cleanse crusted eyes
with magma milk. Dilate portals. Make hear

Jayne Cortez (1934 – 2012), poet, activist, and publisher, was a seminal surrealist innovator whose poetry and jazz recordings were pathbreaking.

Homage

for Elizabeth Catlett Mora

You know us as we are you
creating because impelled
by earth oath and bird cry
womb tie and navel mark
as sure as our parents' pain
our inherited hurt and strength
always Forged by fire, ever constrained
and free, if we understand the certainty
of exclusion from power palaces to which we
will never belong, how our pegs are shaped
differently always, and so ever denied
there Is much to Affirm and ever excluded
there is much to Gather and the Raised fist
asserts and the arm over head Protects
and the sturdy big legs, wide columns below
globe-spanning hips, are Rooted
as eyes large with want and wonder look
skyward searching for what overarches
for all that transcends

*Elizabeth Catlett Mora (April 15, 1915 – April 2, 2012) was
an American-born Mexican sculptor and printmaker. Catlett is
best known for the black, expressionistic sculptures and prints she
produced during the 1960s and 1970s, including "Homage to
Black Women Poets."*

This Time You Were a Man
for Thomas Elias Weatherly II

In your man skin
you made many kin
roped inks   vagrant vagaries
raveled   un   derstood rode
big wheels thru hood reveled
in trope trifles
decon rhythmed rhyme
broke blues   baked song
bread   read   mighty
many tomes Thomas   right
smote   left
all

Thomas Elias Weatherly II, poet, rebel, teacher, was the author of the groundbreaking MauMau American Cantos *and creator of the poetic form, Glory.*

Skinny Poems

for E.L.

He told her she wrote
"those skinny poems"

Wounded child fists pound
within closed city
pummeling concrete
Brooklyn bourgeoisie
yoked to children, men
girdled wild boho
possibilities
familial constraints
circumscribed spirit
reinforced grey doubt
dubious lovers
thieves pilfering joy,
access, sanity

Saved by the writing
soul words punching guts
in rhythmic despair
tympanically blue
affirmations rise

She journeys, arrives
at insight, nearing
seventy, grad school
costly fifth degree
singular among
the merciless young
bleak senselessness of
unpraises stung deep
decades of striving
without critique or
clue shared by those held

dear. misguided pats
on head, false labor
daunting alien
assymetries – count
clap, arhythmically
Soundshapes, delicious
tropes feathered her flight
when she acquired

new tools, she used them
to strike herself to
doubt the insistent
song, still singing true
muffled by distress
to question this blood
beat driving her pen
revelation fell
stunned, stoned, struck, killed her

New Alchemy

for Wifredo Lam

more than michinita
multilingual on the main
diner where skillets dance
deliverance in a chorus
of steaming beans and yellow
rice and green bananas boiled
to fragrant perfections
with soy on linoleum counters
muscling hotsauce here
it is more and less visual
cubanochinita to feel
the pulse of races made warrior
folks who knew the pull of soil
invented hieroglyphs pictograms
characters of mooncurves and skyroofs
words to shake, words to shield, words to steel
bruised heartlands and conscripted cultures

but that then is now. it isn't over
even as you began, it began again,
the rising and the falling
rebirth in the bush and burning in the brush
squid angled and cilla laden spurts of brisk antennae
bristling, waving. here's a code. here's a trail.
here's the mutant body, grab its tale.

polylingual chant of refound
tongues thick with weight of
thickened blood lam lam lam

where young griots trouvère for new city
women in incense laced eventides
play green dolphin streets
with wooden recorders
on the boulevard of dreams lam
gamelon cacophonies of color
address the locus of hydraheaded
hope's fruition exposition and
extradition, lam.
these cool tropics herald you
we replicate your stubborn vision.

> *Wifredo Lam (1902 – 1982) was a Cuban painter, sculptor,*
> *ceramicist and printmaker who sought to portray the enduring*
> *Afro-Cuban spirit and culture.*

Fuel for Beginners
for lisadean

what song did he play
elbow of shadow street lamp
crooklight of dawncool tile
half flight down to echo
angle of horn calling:

every day brings a new tomorrow

Caine-bop sang. Caine
young man, axeslinging hick
from Chi-town
Boonie in duh Big Mac
as in-tosh, apple not peter
nor donald, young armstrong
not Louis and wonder
not Joe or mighty but boy
before mutation of hardtime
fastlife, basement chill and hunger
hit his earnest call that dawn his second day
he played us his unsullied brash dream
i got a song for you

his broadbacked southern accent
one generation from lost
and sobbing sod
is it cold off crying eye
of monster lake waiting to reclaim
its closer shore, o hawk

tell me
tell me
tell me

what song did he play, my friend,
that made us goose and pimple
told you you'd never like him
made me rock and ride and feed
him later feed him
hear about homegirl who'd loved
but couldn't wait more hunger
wandering for a bluer source.

echoing arc of dinged and handsome
subway tile half flight out of lamplight

into muskyroseelectric of silent
village summernight in
mighty mythic youth past
adolescence but possibly prime
plying pennies as you vamped
the babygrand at the surfmaid
i hawked your wares and not
inconsiderable charms as you
and Caine spat the changes

duelled the ascent
up them Giant Steps:
fuel for beginners

tell me what song did he play
before we lost him and each other
in a step closer to believing
it would be all right
and the music would awaken
the sleeping sweet deity
in every ear's inner chamber

What he played before later:
scowled slicked curled furred
gangster moment of his snarling
return, his *"i'll never play in*
smokefilled basements waiting
for a wasting talent to be
drooled over by toothless hags
and fags or scrawled over by
new world blueballs dallying
with license to pen and buttress"
me looking sorry, unpressed

me wishing to play back
that song, if he'd heard it
again, leaping from the mouth
of the cave with the motion
of a thousand errant, fragrant, sturdy wings

all our lives
waiting for a song
we knew to return.

III

Rosa Parks

Sister Rosa
We know you did not just sit down
The myth we made of your act
befogs the potholed road of facts
long journey to your defiance
Your training in nonviolence
in the piney woods
Church sisters furrowing
breaking hard uncivil ground into ready rows
You were not the first choice
to carry this seed
The other less exemplary could not withstand white scrutiny
if shoved into national lights
dismissible shameable in her single motherhood
o! how wise sisters understood.
You were impeccable
impermeably good
and married and golden
The truth far grander than fatigue
that our struggle strategized in word and deed
more than outburst
more than anger
more than one hot day's insult or need
that patient steady planning knows the hunger it must feed
and image Davids must sling
through the giant's ugly head
Guided oh guided by praying dreamers
singing out to God
ready from within

Hairdressers

I

Girl, she told me
watch out for those mens with pictures
of other women on they
tall oak chest of drawers
when you ask they be saying
Nah, her, she's just an old
something. but you better know
better know better know
nothing dead remains at eye level.

II

The dapper esthetician
rubbed her face with herbs
scraped scales and reprimanded
"drink water by the quart not the teaspoon"
"some people" he pouted, "don't know
how to behave." he was waiting
in chrome and steel coloredhood
on the east side so folks could go down
or over in his white coat and french skills
for a star to lie beneath his heatlamps

III

The big one chopped my hair.
He could flutter thick fingers
like a raffia breeze swore
betty was carmen 'cause he knew his jazz
and bemoaned brenda russell's passing. that music
ooo, into prince. but really travelled
away. the partypeople pursued
a lesser dream. All the men he'd
love were us, honey, 'cause the
others, you don't know where they've been

IV

Readying first wrench back
to fryhood down the hill to harlem proper. where
the westindian woman wore a gold tooth
in a razor smile honey can i
help you she tried to steal
me before my lady returned
from back and the man wearing a peacoat
and a suitcase full of outsize girdles

appeared. all the old women gathered
like pigeons to wonderbread in mount morris park
the old yellow woman would be burnt
by the old yellow woman
the razor smiles and broke souls
went to bigbreasted goldtooth who'd bandy or browbeat
each client fit her lady
pets to their owners each
booth was an office an altar
to stringent god of grease and hot iron
and the serious or those passing through
went to my lady of second car,
home in jersey
each head a step
toward freedom

V

Lola gentled fiveyearold cries
my tenderheaded strain
against the comb
lessened
sometimes her belly against my head
but she had a way
better than mommy's
somewhere close to barbering:
sober grownups in tilefloored splendor
of mirror facing streetlife see
yourself in grand high chairs
spinning thrones pedaled upwards
to attending angels of beauty's ministry
her apartment up the hill
St. Nicholas Avenue in Harlem
large dark calm space
devoted to chasten me pretty
mommy said you must
suffer for beauty

VI

Andy gave it the old college try
reinitiated me to chemical fry
a little richard
the old time religion
in the hang of his conked
dark locks
the rigor of his hysteria
that vocal sweep from chuckle to giggle
tattle-tale sans tit

had shampooed and straightened
3 generations 2 sides of family
some of all were there to cry over him
he was going when he last did me
conked my hair to a tee

VII

The one too serious
to be gay too nervous to be
messing in my head with heat
the one they'd call queer and rob
or faggot and rape on a twilit
summer evening below series of shuteyed lampposts
or just take his day's earnings
why else would his musty shop
bear signs of botanica or
air of funeral parlor, purple maroon
velvet drapes heavy with lashes and wide sashes
windowbox clotted w persistent upper growth of dead plants
why else would he be on '16th street
smack traffic central
denizens of despair
prowling daynight sidewalks
for hydrants of anything to be uncapped
why else would he do my hair
urge me home rush me out of there

VIII

Lalonnie, for hawaiian birth
(her mommy reshaped the spelling),
tugged my naps to freedom from
the daily scrape of comb
array of braids, carefree corona
lanky nimbus walking
with ease swimming with joy
bounded variations of millipath
threads, deft weave of future
and past, the taut pull and
facelift, headtingling tug
and slant-eyed stretch of scalp:
low tech and high craft
magic midwife attending pain
and crowning glories
made me love my head
let my sweat be welcome again.

46

The first time I heard

the word used on me: Laurelton   New York
1963   as i made my way
home from PS 156   never heard it

in that sweet South Bronx in the fifties or
those first years of the sixties   i knew it
from watching fire hosed German shepherd
seized children on TV   i   knew it as

it landed on my ears as i dodged stones
and placards, saw angry, ugly face house-
wives chanting that we should not be there
we weren't 4th, 5th, 6th graders anymore

running to Merrick Boulevard, running
to the bus, traveled for Intellectually
Gifted Children, Opportunity Classes

in this land of lawn, garages, grills, backyards,
one-family homes, our own tree-filled streets
we weren't boys & girls we were besieged,
we became one & we were black & we

asked each other across grades & classes:
whose mothers were these? none of them
recognizable, none of their children
smart enough to sit next to us

Hubert and Teddy

I did not have a word for what they promised
– a special kind of pain
those brothers hunted, tracked me
for reasons I still don't understand
miles outside the neighborhood
to the Laurelton library where my mind lived
awaited my departure at closing to threaten me

They lived in the Dead End
in a better house, so I rejoiced a bit
when my brother said they came to naught
drugged, insensate, grown wide
on their mother's plastic-covered couch

What if someone had stopped them
back when the dirt streets were malleable
before my book bag became another weapon
before I had to fight black boys, too.

Duck and Cover

Before the South Bronx became a brown Dresden
before I was stoned going home from school
before I ever heard the N-word
before Martin Luther King, Jack and Robert Kennedy were assassinated
before my grandmother died and the store closed
before we moved away from everything that gave me independence to the
        strange bourgeoisie of queens
before we were poor among the middle-class
before we were hip among the country
before I planted my first corn went to Jamaica wore a bra or got my period
before my sister was born and our uncle died after defeating drugs
before drugs blazed new trails up young noses and along young veins
before people slept piled up in Macy's side doors
We were told that an evil Empire might send world-killing bombs
that would melt us by their de-creating light
We were told to curl into a ball and face the wall
to cover our necks and faces
We had to look good even if we were fried.

Rebirth

She won't remember but we older siblings do
how she blew all our minds with past life stories
that she told Daddy while we were in school

Daddy worked nights, was her day care and knew
how to brush hair, cajole and entertain his babies
She won't remember but we older siblings do

Certain old French songs made her cry, others made her coo
Some reminded of misfortunes, others recalled great deeds
This she told Daddy while we were in school

There was no way she could know such things so it had to be true
She still saw and would regale us with past glories
She won't remember but we older siblings do

She said the Big Bang was how the universe grew
Someone named Donna, some street life tragedy
that she told Daddy while we were in school

Her baby self would dance an ancient hootchie-coo
an adult and piercing wisdom when she was only three
She won't remember but we older siblings do
what she told Daddy while we were in school

The Phyllis Wheatley Poetry Festival 1973

Thank God, Alma was with you
as you stood waiting for a taxi
in front of the hotel in Jackson, Mississippi.
She snatched you back
before you fired your New York mouth
at cruising old white men
soliciting rage. Not one car, but three.
Couldn't they see your pillar-high gélé,
regal West African boubou meant that maple flesh
was not on parade, was not for sale?

Soon you would gather again
with other daughters of Phyllis Wheatley,
celebrate a new history with your pens,
over 100 years of legal literacy.
Alma, country sophomore from Tennessee,
knew something. How to wait for the next moment

in this town that slaughtered its college students
as you were, sprung from bleak, Berkshire Billsville
to a warm November evening frosted with this reminder:
how suddenly you could be snatched out of you
as others were, just a year before. 'Let's not die tonight
on a humble, all they see is black pussy standing still.'
Her small hand strong on your big arm,

and this not all you know of Jackson, its south:
Emmett Till, Chaney, Goodman, Schwerner,
german shepherds leaping at little black girls,
bombed churches, fire hoses, lynchings,
innocence always trampled or smashed by greed.
Alma holds back your need to protest,
lengthening your life past nineteen.

The Wall Beyond Rage

that certitude is a death
does not dissuade the frantic search of many
does not deter donning its blind veil, gagging shroud or
coffin-armor before promise is recognized or decoded

that certitude is the real opiate
routine is syringe and anarchy is not antidote
only a holding pattern against a landing submission
then surges rage as dim-eyed, hungered and weary
we clutch the fragile myths to fragment.
the litter cannot bear the restless
agony of labor swelling – dancing, pumping, knifing, rising
kicking screaming cursing shouting
shouting to the wall.

the cunning intellectuals congratulate arrival
carve a doctrine of dogma: the tenets of arrival
that arrival is a death
does not defuse its fervent celebration
does not disrobe its priests, unravel mystique
or alarm spent anger to awaken

the terrain beyond each temporal truth we crave, beckons
yet craven, we fashion walls against the perilous country
only one moment beyond this, we live. cessation is
surrender. the only prize the journey.

IV

Soil

Don't they know those not born to it love it more,
cherish it like converts to a foreign faith
hold its wisdom precious, perish for its lack?
It's not in the speech around us
so we study its language with rigor:

My grandparents kept it in many pots crowding windows,
my parents acquired it
so that I could, earlier than they,
later than my sapling siblings,
have some to dream on.

I wanted to be farmer
before I was to be oceanographer, meta-lawyer, mother.
The short corn was taller than preteen me,
alien kohlrabi, bush beans, tomatoes
celebrated as miracle by apartment-reared parents
who praised my scrawny crops.

Tell the gawking this as they watch me tend my garden
Tell them black folks tilled much soil
even as we left it, we hid seeds in cheek pockets,
saved core of alligator pears
and guarded the eyes of tubers.

We carried it even as we fled it.
Tell them I grew up with radiator arboretums,
mayonnaise jar composts of eggshell water
and spent coffee grounds,
steam heat hothouses, fire escape forests
and tenement window hillsides,
avocado trees singing tropical songs above the guttered snow.

Tell them I don't need their bad advice.
I know.

Plant

I

Your people fled the place to plant
because they needed to grow beyond rows
back breaking hoes, feudal rule

where labor is conscripted by conspiracies of privilege
"Those farm boys hate their farms," the Korean vet said

and quick quick generations leap up and away
multiplying in concrete verticalities, losing earth wisdom
in bleak struggles to meet different debtors

Some of your people stay
place holding, as long as they
are able to meet new taxes
stave off vetch creep of agribusiness
big tooled, lawyered, politricked out
carrying minor magistrates in their back pockets
using commissioners like tobacco
to be smoked or chewed in service of acquisition

yet your people fight for minor turf
mortgaging possibilities of illusory privilege
while down home crumbles. Lapses in paying taxes
means wide green lessons gone
summer migrations of blackbird children
where once they learned those lessons beyond street.
Lost.

Not always for lack of understanding
small farms under siege everywhere round this world
black farms threatened with doubled forces
of conspiring desires. They want your land.
They got a big money plan for it.
They want your land. How dare you own it.
What 40 not bottled? What mule?

II

Everywhere big agriculture tricked out like military.
Machineries of making, scaling nutrition out,
sucking water tables from under others, making wells run dry,
diverting rivers to feed orange groves
that another you will never own,
only pick in, or flee, to some gray city

and those of you who
yam the greens picking over picked produce
as if you knew it,
and you want to say who grew it?
You once grew it until growing got mechanized,
routinizing unpredictabilities by manipulating genes.
Then who grew it, attack-resistant
impervious to insect, perfect and unreal?

III

You, only second generation away
from dawn's mango perfume,
sun combing fog off St. Ann's blue mountains
those fled them backbreak, hard persistence of heavy duty always
something to feed, clean, move, tend,
and days from barely see to can't
and yet you want some of it back,
somehow you need it.

IV

all green does not yield green
as do plantain, dandelion, gill over the ground
or ground ivy snaking tendrils under fence
and carrot before becoming Queen Anne's Lace
young milkweed before flowering, before monarch's munch
burdock before burr is bloom-full, fiber rich
and that early spring white-flowered stalk thing

with green of green near pea green
which says a soupçon of yellow but not, is garlic mustard
savory invader whose leaves may salad or garnish sandwich
and whose stalks yield another green with some olive to it
when you've cooked and beaten it to a pulp for paper
feeding your words after your body
and where are words as the Inuit have for snow
how many ways to show you each green?

V
You crouch sweating and dirt-dirty
so clean dirty and so cleansed eh?
not the filth of concrete street nor piss nor strangers' feces

No. These feces you know. possum pass. bat guano
pigeon poop, bird squirt bring new green thing
that white poppy mallow of matisse leaves, furred tongue centers
You smell neighbor cat's incursion and skunk warning
and still the danger of sky booms bursting upon you

and something falling from it or wind whirl
sweeping you up and weather is less alien
as you scratch in your little patch and dream of acreage
your singular colored self some strange astonishment
to children untutored to possibilities of their greenness
they may revile their tame kerchiefs of broken wilderness
and know it only as thing to keep trim by noisy machine
to push or ride

so bandannaed, rucksacked in lines
of laboring color you could be understood
but in forgetful twitch of historic amnesia
not in this neighborhood?
as with spade you unearth the lesson contained
in those mayonnaise water jars of crushed shells
and spent coffee grounds your grandfolk
kept to feed their window jungles and fire-escape forests
in those huge pots of purchased dirt holding trees grown
from eaten alligator pear, other sprouting smuggled bits
of home

planting.

Fruit Stand

Just plucked plums
memories of Half Moon Bay
new gray house near ocean
fruit stand on sand-brushed road
San Gregorio –
an arid place with lots of water
past sunflowers and pumpkins
out of New York's season
along the narrow winding road
from Belmont over to the sea.

Here, on River Road,
where tiny city melts to country
on the left when leaving
on the right when coming home
is a sign and call to stop and eat
fresh, fresh from flat land you drive by

When Daddy defended the apples his father sold
in another century, by concrete
below tall buildings
he recalls in his dimming brightness
a fruit stand, a place for products of earth unaltered
to be purchased, protected, stolen, desired
gathered there to be gotten
to be eaten, to be fed.

Why must we go away to see what waits
around green corners and down bright blocks:
shepherds' coveted, covered fleece in Painted Post
bee keepers' fresh honey in Watkins Glen
glorious garlic grown by postman farmer
squash bounties from many gardens
the plain heart tug of hand-written signs
to slow down, stop and savor
delight on our own slender roads.

Acknowledgment
for Albert Howe

Young blood   spice blood   flame blood   of youth frantic
disbelief in mortality's course or its personal touch
run sly and close to building's shelter
against the predatory rain of beebees
precocious graduate to dream turned lethal

His first dead man a déja vu
not dime movie glamour no soft focus
Buick slow gravity yielding to crush
a worker's chest whose struggle to maintain
became a bubble of blood   like spittle in mouth
chest coughing out its ruddy phlegm
street run red   so easy street run red life gurgles
street run red   no blessing in this baptism

Thrice chastisement schools struck then
fierce corporeal agendas to chasten
strong colts would bear a future saddle
slow ox would bear the yoke, or die in battle
The blows, the whips, the wooden paddle
control young engines' surge with ruler
remind of inches, never miles
mind parameters, shape the heathen wild

Parents reinforced the sanctioned agenda:
newspaper on floors for spit polish sheen
of Sunday parlors adorned with obsequious lace
cloying bric-a-brac beauty
frail enchantments within their hard scheme of duty
scaled to fit cold water flat's space
not living rooms where his boxed ears squirmed
sunday sunday torture to culture
within the screech of ancient sopranos
trilling colonial renderings of art.

Ritual remnants
money in corners, an unnamed retention
shrapnel fetish of motherland's flesh dismembered
ambivalence of church to spirit realm visitations
obeisance to unwritten laws remembered:
use cobwebs under sink 'cause root an herb
no where to be gathered
Montserrat! home relations, imported pieces

of the healing arts contorted
fit industrial landscapes better

His was second generation thrust by first
patrician dictates, peasant flight
to an urban village where mothers' cries
fall from tenement windows and all recognize
whose son you are, thrice chastised
school street home thrice shame
for obstreperous behavior and real pain
stifled below a trembling preparation for man

rivertimes   heedless fishing in the romance of his loins
rivertimes   harlem swimming in the life of his age
rivertimes   dirty water dip joy, slice the shimmering cool
defy and chase and plunge and flow

asphalt beach for tender feet
down the slope from Sugar Hill
when all Harlem boulevards strove
free from peasant destiny

That time of shine, smart awnings
when Harlem scrubbed her steps, swept her streets
when people slept on rooftops
unguarded while the summers raged

Hunger was companion and need was mate
Sold apples for a nickel, protect his father's store
with badge of gang fight daily for respect
To say survivor doesn't mean you forget

the practicum of death in early years
Boys play war when men embrace despair
Called themselves the Buccaneers
bombed the pants of parkbench drunk
Ha! Lit up! They'll never know

Grew quickly tall, later, short
an adolescent edge on age
access to the swiftlife joints
where the grownup children played

Recall what should have never been but was
Dope's premiere generational claim
Friends crucified on a hypodermic cross
The only excused, burnt at ignorance's stake

He watched the snake
but didn't crawl on his belly.

(was birthed at home by cousin Price
a real m.d. and two nurse attendants
Money from folks for his nativity
another afrikan retention

So much under mother's pillow
It was pinned to Christmas tree
bore his mother's name, youngest of three
had plenty money on his natal tree.)

Scion of matrilineal nobility and
paternal genius beyond soil's demand
small turf for a mind expanding:
Albert was a race man

Older, learned the greater scheme
of Culture, Conscience, Language, Need
Mother's Zion, Garvey's creed
Father's peach pies, fiddle and mandolin

Goat don't bring sheep

He danced the old world and the new:
Calypso, tap and mess around
Hucklebuck and Susie Q, waltzed and latined too
He dug the cool artifice of urban dude

The music that went with all of that
grew when bebop sprang from swing
Knew all the tunes when Pres was King
Sang the riffs, knew how to scat

Talked the many tongues of harlem
Walked the sharp dress, lean and slick
Slung the words, his silent laughter
Caught sweet flowerings of swift chicks

Sent to die again, to War
as before him, Kinsmen fought
again safeguard land that held them hostage
human chattel in gilded cage

Democracy, Imperialism's rationale rode high
on the victory of that second war's broken tide
even if his conscience could object
Harlem's status, second class, couldn't hide

had no college to protect
He left a sergeant, mechanic ace tinker, tool wise
Honorable Discharge from a gruesome mission
he'd work to forget

Some compensation : mainstream entry
benefits for Korean vets

Lost his buckteeth in defense of a nation
that breaks the swiftlimbed youth to hobble
defangs the ravenous minds of young cats
Returned to civil service south of Harlem

> *young colts would learn to bear the saddle*
> *slow ox the yoke, or die in battle.*

Lacked support and pedigree
that buys spare time
When asked what things he could create
he'd say "I play the dial" and smile

He dreamt machines that came to be
Drafted sounds' new carriage and shape
His schema wore an earnest genius
but never got his college degree

The rumor of his throw-back might
mouthing called to liberty's quiet battles
Maiden seduced him, unicorn with innocence
The town surrounded and cast the net

He married his Hope, balm in Gilead
ripe gourd for homefilling desires
Matched heart's scope and breadth
quelled his restless wild to rest

Two daughters, one son, together they bore three
souls to learn their legacy: They who fight
and run away, live to fight another day
Teach the children to fight and pray

As he would, empty cupboard nights
of makeshift meals, his children's evergrowing needs
spare them some of life's raw deals
"O Father," intercessor for his plight
"Help me smelt a brighter destiny
from these canyons of steel, find some malleable vision."
He'd kneel at inner altar, "O Father! Help me carve
a safer place, survive a white world's derision."
Tears silent as his laughter

Sigh and rise. Kiss us on our cheeks and eyes
His "crazy crew" would wait beyond bedtime
to kiss their laboring hero goodbye
"Dance, Daddy, Dance," his youngest would yell
He'd click his heels to signify he was well
Testimony to spirit's facility to smile
He'd leap three times until out of sight
Stride toward civil service' night-shift hell

What's that cat's name he would muse
the one with innards plucked and doomed
to push his burden, never ending
his constant, constant, constant abuse

Deep sigh and rise...
Some other myth to feather his flight
one of mind's supremacy over matter
He'd at least change the type of battle
he'd angle a less demeaning barter

Teach the children how to maneuver
Grow his crop a little better
Arm them let them have a childhood
and encourage new wing testing

Spared them some of his mistakes
Shared his handsome heart's full measure
Love: his only unassailable treasure
Never forget the time he swore
he'd break his son's legs before
he'd ever let him be taken for war

or how he struggled to resist
western canons of male chauvinist
the daughter could express mechanical interests
received for christmas toys which taught
robot and microscope assembly kits

"The women of this family
are a strong demanding breed
when your mother decides, I best take heed
She's got a Mind you know
knows things I'll never know."

Or how he sometimes failed
Boy never got the dolls he craved
those plastic warmen that would wage
mock battles on a child's developing stage

Who knows? He wonders if he did it right
Wonders how to have done it better
Wonders how much he should have passed on
of the world's disintegrating horrors...

But then again, my daddy
was a race man and i was
spared primary confusions and misapprehensions
He taught me to jump our double dutch:
twin ropes of consciousness encircling
to enter at appropriate moments
lift legs, spin and twirl as sure
as walking, to do the necessary,
and when blind sweat signalled
your energy's expiration,   leave.

Dementia

I

I am preparing for his forgetting
how could he not invite me to his wedding
where were the answers to my gifts and cards
lost in crumbling synapses, burning of bridges,
rigidizing brain

Yesterday I was furiously doggy paddling
a stroke he taught, to stay afloat
as briny waves smack you silly
Today stepmother said, 'dementia'
and I am grateful for something else to blame

In the language he once commanded
whirl the mighty round toward some more equitable move,
my father's grandiloquence is hobbled by a 'how do you say?'
masked by cunning subject changes, astute silences,
wisdom wisping away as soon as it arrives
Neither his mind nor body leaps and click heels
three times, as he would for us, when nightshifting our passage
to better lives

I prod him again to talk into a tape recorder

> Hot mickeys in the cold concrete winter, tap dancing
> apple selling, apple stealing, horse drawn wagons fruit
> sellers singing up to high tenement windows his mother
> florrie's shakespearean admonitions pool halls fights the
> make out flat he shared with some buddies while living at
> home all that music in his mind from lunceford, gaillard,
> the five cats, king oliver, connie kay was down the block
> with folks from the same down-the-way ooo, countee
> cullen's lessons, aviator high school, megamythic streets

can't remember all his stories, his tests, majestic jazz lineages
Stepmother thinks youthful head knockings loosened something
now unstuck. Says they spoiled him. 'ol big head Albe'
We thought his gang time and dysfunctional siblings
whose pieces he picked up again and again
meant he was toughened and roughened
and in the same mystic Harlem gift,
smoothed to articulate and dapper perfection

II
What did I tell my friend Ira –
as his mother's words, pirouettes and ikebana bouquets,
became wheelchaired, halting, daisy chained
wilting in piss death stench of twelve grand a month nursing home
ignored by New York's latest immigrants yearning to breathe free

Something cogent and true
useless in the face of growing graceless:
just be in the moment
when she knows you a bit and tells you in cinematic detail
of a life ended before you were born,
before world wars, before she spoke only English
before America, before Canada was a place you might need to
escape to, how her father's furs made wealth in Montreal,
how their divorce made her poor

When did you get your cats? I ask another friend,
You must remember everything that doesn't hurt
scrub aware every forgetful moment with practice
learn something new, crosswords, acupuncture, dissent

III
My huge, expensive, birthday card
says I'm a piece of his brain his body has not yet undone
but his lefty's 45-degree-angled
slanting, crisp print-script is cloudy, rounded

only the word, Love, looks sort of the same
signing his name, not his Daddy title
Has he forgotten who he is to me
only remembering that half a century ago
something special happened?

"Tell her thank you for the call"
I hear stepmother directing him
Did he forget why he dialed?
"Dahlin, dahlin, thank you. Love you like crazy."

You must remember everything that doesn't hurt.

At the Renny

Son, come dance with me
they playing jump up music

And the mammoth woman would wear him out
dancing to those 15-minute songs
fueled by that over Overproof firewater
they'd be drinking
and the need to stomp
Not at the Savoy
where conkheaded hicks
lindy-ed and bucked for tourists
fingering the edge of blank coins
but at The Renny
where Don Wilson and his stalwarts
would lay down a hipspinning, legtwirling rhythm

singing a West Indian muddled into Spanish
and these thickheavy women would
rise from behind mounds
of fried chicken, bowls of rice 'n peas
warm pots of fragrant steaming greens
up to meet the music's lust throated call

and grab him, this thin man
and dance the life, strong, fierce
out of, into him.

Dancing on Daddy's Feet

He was our brown Fred Astaire
thin, dashing, fleet-footed hero
time stepping, sand shuffling
tapping, twirling
doing that click toe touch up our stairs

elegant line from head to finger
or shoulderwinged back architected moves
lindying, shimmying, hip swung glides
watching our grooves, showing precedent slides

He taught us:
  Buck and Bubbles
      think through troubles
  Nicholas Brothers
      heed your family and not others
  Bill Bojangles Robinson
      though they steal your song
         sing on

Saved all his deft skill for us
Daddy could dance so many ways
He would lend me his grace:
let me place small flat feet on his
and hold my hands, smiling
would show me where to step

as if I could ever learn
to do it backwards and in heels
as if I could ever learn his strength

Montserrat

Montserrat!
I am your daughter outsider
daughter outsider
yankee come home
searching debris
for a history lost to lava
for a surviving kernel

for place where Grandma Florrie
stood in de fork of road
waiting for her daddy
tell him how they mistreat she
those six older sisters
where she brought she half-sister
home with a *look who I find*
and was beaten for her
innocent impropriety

Montserrat,
what grows inna land reclaimed by lava?
how can I learn my lineage
without tree or road, shack or industry
the knowing in the land burnt or buried under ash
no burial ground, no ghosts
and no people to school me

why me kin dreamt dreams
that sailed them away to this country
of chilling hostilities and grey concrete
hard streets rather than lime sleep
emerald sing, azure eat, perfume see

I am of the Albert of the Lucretia of the Howe
and Samuel known as Big Dan of the Whites
I say she first
because how it be among them –
woman determined lineage
like back in Sierra Leone
and men wandered

if you look like me, let me know.

Soufrière Speaks

searching debris / for a history lost to lava

what crawls at my feet
what land is my meat
what heart is my heat
naming does not contain me
Lava licks earth with scorch tongue ardor
Me lava wipes earth with desire's erasure
I undo you too I come unbidden heaving rock
running in stately streams of sunforce

August 3, 1997
Pyroclastic flows from Soufrière Hills volcano on
Montserrat ~~have~~ reached ~~the~~ capital city ~~of Plymouth.
Many~~ homes and businesses can be seen burning from
~~several~~ miles away. Fire fighters ~~have been~~ unable
to stop these flames which threaten ~~to consume~~ the
entire city. ~~Flows in Gages Valley have also caused
fires in Gages Village.~~ These flows generated ash
plumes ~~which reached elevations of~~ over 15,000 ft
~~(4500 m).~~ Ashfalls ~~occurred in Isles Bay, Ole Towne,
Salem and several other areas west of the volcano.
In the wake of this event and a~~ June 25 event ~~which~~
left 10 dead and nine others missing, ~~the~~ British
government is considering permanently relocating all
of Montserrat's citizens off the island.

Magma, what beneath the earth
undersea, at root at core
Fireheart of all unknowing
not angry, flameheart not beating
yet seething with nameless need for release
Me geyser   me spray   me spit   hot earth under earth
earth below your eyes beyond your knowing
earth under bone long snake snaking   all names gone

August 16, 1997
~~An increase in activity has prompted authorities to
expand the exclusion zone and~~ offer residents money
and transportation to neighboring islands. ~~Details
such as the exact amount of money to be offered and
who will be offered the deal have yet to be disclosed.
In the meantime, the~~ governor of Monserrat ~~has~~ ordered
~~the~~ evacuation of towns ~~of Flemings, Hope, Olveston,
and Salem before~~ nightfall, ~~citing a report by the
Montserrat Volcano Observatory that the central part of~~
the island is in more danger than previously thought

Me belly burp   me belly groan   me belly laugh   me belly moan
All flee before me relentless upsurge
flowing over island to hiss in sea no hose extinguish me
this hot cold wrath no trench divert my path
tree bow before me, turn to ash
metal buckle even treasure, even trash disappear
heat of me heat   be implacable cool   feel nothing
but move to rule no kith to me   no kin you name me
under brother
No brethren we

<pre>
October 2, 1997
Three more explosions occurred over the last 24 hours.
~~Each of these explosions were~~ followed by pyroclastic
flows down all sides of the volcano. Flows of pumice
and ash reached the sea ~~through the Tar River valley~~
~~and White River valley. They also reached farms,~~
~~Dyer's and Plymouth. The large~~ amount of material
deposited ~~on the volcano during this activity~~ allows
each subsequent flow to travel farther. Eruption
columns rose to heights of 20,000 to 40,000 ~~ft after~~
~~each explosion.~~ Ash and pumice clasts up to almost 1
inch ~~(~2 cm) in diameter has~~ fallen on inhabited areas
of Montserrat ~~from these explosions.~~
</pre>

And I am my own entry my own exit
I have ended your green generations
with my scorch jism my megasquirt my blood flow scalds
my voice rumbles, roar of earth shudder, tremble twitch
Earth birthing earth, shedding earth, earth itch
earth scratch, stretch I awaken I roam reach I range,

And I is not I, nor one, nor here, the is that I am is below
everywhere, roiling, circling so this is just pinch,
just surface just a rising a raising a yawn without purpose
an earth belch, a popped granite zit, a cleansing after sleep,
ablution reclaiming land, my land me, I reclaim me land
was/is never yours, it is mine, it is me, you are gone
tree shriek grass calls for goat, for sheep
for that which eats but not unroot.

October 1, 2002
Volcanic and seismic activities at Soufrière Hills
~~have been~~ high since September 20th. ~~On the 21st, a~~
spine grew ~~in the central region of the dome and~~
~~growth in the NE stagnated.~~ ~~On the evening of the~~
~~25th,~~ generation of pyroclastic flows begin on the
western flank as the dome growth shifted ~~to this~~
~~side.~~ ~~A~~ large lobe ~~was~~ observed the next morning.
~~The~~ eruptive activity ~~then changed again towards the~~
~~north and a~~ low-level ash cloud ~~was~~ emitted ~~in the~~
~~afternoon of the 29th.~~ This cloud was observed the
next day over E Puerto Rico ~~by satellite imagery. On~~
~~the evening of the 29th,~~ a pyroclastic flow, ~~with an~~
~~estimated~~ volume of 2 to 3 million ~~m3,~~ went down the
northern flank and reached the sea.

I de root red root deep source before flesh living flesh
rooting deeper than ancestry life before genes before DNA
snatch and twisty speck of me. Aaaaaaaaaaaaaaa me first
ehhhhhhhhh me last rrrrrrrrrrrrrrrrrrrrrrrrrrrrrrrrrrrrrrr
glass and furnace, fire and cauldron
hills awakened to mount to mountain to pumping within
what was hidden must come out must come out must
come flying flailing wailing out out out
must leap up up up all that was hidden must stretch under
pressure must terraform must realign must redesign must
burn must melt must ash must float away must move must
earthbirth must must be revealed

The Them Gone

I had not been home since her funeral
Her husband, my father, alone for seven months
was already dating and that Fathers' Day weekend
he was overexcited
asking me ten times what he should cook.

As if he had not cooked for me a million times before:
              when he had the night shift, undertook the domestic
              with varying degrees of palatable
              not like her cuisine, always manna:
              his liver, bacon, onions,
              ketchup for everything, steak-blood gravies
              spurred me to cook at 12.

As if he had to do anything.

But this was our first time alone together
our first time without mommy
just out of ear shot, at her sewing machine
shopping in the city, on her way
she, whom I only grudgingly shared.

She was the one I wanted to remain.

Maybe he was afraid of me, their first experiment.
He was Igor without his scientist, the one who kept control
and knew all the formulas for regeneration.
So lonely here, he said he could feel her sometimes.

I couldn't.

He was the sudden widower with *"those damn bitches*
who didn't wait till she was cold in the grave before calling"
a wacky misstatement since she was cremated
not what she wanted
but who could argue
with this wild man ripped from his moorings
bereft of his beloved after 44 faithful years
of growing, settling, nurturing the kind of passion
that made old boyfriends bring their new women
to witness the unbelievable tender of their joy:
rubbing her hurt feet unashamedly in public.

Songs he could no longer sing to her or us
my blue heaven, when I move on the outskirts of town
words he would no longer say: *moosh, moosh, moosh, Hopie, dahlink*
her name   his happy shout up the stairs: HOPE.

Retired from his steep 35-year ascent
in this small Queens A-frame house she never wanted
but made home, with brilliant buys gathered one by one
the mirrored oak armoire, those plush gold
velvet high-back chairs.

Left with their first hatchling on Fathers' Day
who broke their wedded bliss into family
who as a teen pecked his super hero shell to see
suddenly just a man, a father, *next time I'll have wombats*
and like Twain, I rethink him brilliant again.

Facing him in bright glare of kitchen light
feeling the enormity of his loss of the love of his life
his best friend, companion, beloved wife
something I have yet to have and hold.
Learning what was her, what was him, what was
us, what was *them*.

My own gut whacking yawp of mother-robbed grief
swallowed shut as together we
                        chopped the onions
                        found tamari to marinate the fish
                        shredded Boston bibb, grated ginger,
                        chopped carrots,
touched all her spices, made a meal.

First Drunk

The guys had a keg or a barrel of wine,
MD 20-20, rot gut, no better than 4 roses,
something they hid by the Long Island railroad track,
moved at least twice weekly in '69, told me about,
which emerged to enter the punch at
Cyrus' debut bacchanal in his mother's
basement, our first party. His older
sisters helped, we screwed red light bulbs in
sockets, decorated, gathered 45s,
my father drove me over, he would
pick me up at 11 after I had
drunk the punch again and again and
learned ten minutes with the Vietnam
vet throbbing on my pelvis as we
dipped deeply, swiveled to "Stay in My
Corner" STAY, until Cyrus yelled, "What
are you doing?!" Threw a coat on us,
turned on headlights, stopped the music, chastised,
rushed me upstairs to drink coffee, wash
my flushed transformed face with cold water,
wish away cat eyes, a new irrevocable
sign that I was high. "He was Blind!"
"Couldn't tell in the dark," I laugh, shake,
try to get straight before Daddy
came to get me.

First Kiss

Did i kiss "Uncle" Jack in front of
everybody? his furry chest and fine face
mommy said i embarrassed her
as i touched him blissful,
oblivious,   innocent in my lust
made my daddy sad   already   his
3-year old dreamt of other loves

Or was it Tony i wanted
in a way i had no name for
my stomach hula-hooping
did my godmother know
how grateful when her son
tied my orthopedic shoes
as if lacing slippers, i felt
as he peeked up my dress
as if there was anything to see
o yes o yes he was green lantern
and i said the oath fervent in the dark
to fight evil   something sweet happened
because my brother told

Won't count my cousin's furry tongue
yechy under the sheet tent to show me
how.   strange   nasty   she could hide
gum in her mouth   always was fast
burning tracks as she smoked through
life as if i needed to know anything she knew

Wasn't glib George until college
nor tall Stewart or articulate Jerry
or randy Rodney, they all refused my
pretty, curly, eager bows. first drunk
grinding in Cy's basement
with that blind 'Nam vet yet no kiss.

'Til tawny, lionmaned, tennis-playing Ira
his congas and our shared ideals
and how did it happen in that angry
new time we spent demonstrating
redefining crying growing and leaving
home he leaned over   turned his
head sideways and held me and

i held him, hungry for tomorrow
believing we would die in a hale
of bullets in a revolution never come.
Stealing touches, drinking urgent nectars
pressed in the corner by the band room
after i returned my bassoon.

I Shed 185 Pounds Writing Poetry

Lighter than me, he was still too much to carry,
my wings couldn't lift us and he refused
to yield to the itch by his shoulders
though I caressed his feet with lavender
and massaged his shins with almond oil
brought ice and heat for his spasms, pulled
and sucked his fingers, none of my rubbing
or watering made him sprout. Instead, I broke
into blossom, flooding every bed we knew
finally washing him out.

Simple As That

you dismiss heartache like it's all forewent
and yeah some tarry, carrying world weights
on god fitted shoulders, ignoring "ist"
vultures plucking gut-bits
like blond locks on Hendrix licks,
little winging it played flat.
it matters that some take their heartache to the world stage,
purging every other other for their lack of love,
waging death, and others just kill
parents, cousins, neighbors for immediate relief
my heartache means my last eggs
will drop unpierced and unflowering,
a whole generation of all i had to give and teach
will not even be ghosts.
why good men weren't born?
because my heartache didn't bear them
those meant-for-me's died in war or were imprisoned
and the make-dos didn't make it
and i tell you i was right to cry at 19 for arrogant actor who ran home to Texas,
dropping out of college, and i was right to cry at 29 for freaky writer
with 3 kids, learning later only one was his
i was right to mourn at 39 the death of my marriage
to jealous academic who lied about wanting children
and i'm crying now for my last eggs creaking over mountains
broke in my hand, fried on hot guitar skillet of wandering compu-buddhist
and i tell you, i knew each chance was golden
i get to cry 'cause i wasted none of it
and loved from red to gold to blue to purple
with my matter and all my subtle bodies
and this heartache keeps me from organizing
and this heartache keeps me from joy
and this heartache makes the roar of the world louder and louder
words all bleed together and moment is always a splinter under my finger
flayed skin grabbing grit, unsealing wounds with each balmy Sunday
watching luck-blessed families embrace
recalling the glory of that tiny childhood house
where two in love made three
and all we wanted most was each other, safely home.

v

my mother is an indictment
i am fettered by the genes
limited before beginning
i cry against her
that she was not more
than second generation running
from that tropic tongue
too chastised to be fast
too whipped to be hip
not bold enough to embrace
heartrhythm's wilderness
spice nights of peas 'n rice
the lingolilt of her people
persisting after backs dry
and green ripen
like banana   like guava
like mango   comesome
gingerbeer burn in mouth

little blackgirl runningfasthard breathless
beyond sweat her braids loosening in flight
running (*monkee monkee monkee chaser*)
hurled wordspears falling short
of flailing black legs   *monkee chaser*
tribe silver on her arm marking her
as sure as cheekscars *monkeechaser* she stop
hard turns shescared shefight flailing arms
of fear fight strong with fear fatigue she fight
she strong   shechange   shebecome

yankeegirl   accentless
Harlemcool and homegrownsweet
she nocookhot this second generation
she no jibe-jive with elders
in accented imitation no
she run fast she run fast
slicing off edges   cutting her mythical tail
collecting menstrual blood
offerings for the melting pot
idol of her parent's new religion
multistoried monstrosity with fool's
gold pasties on witch's marquee
beautiful at the distance   unbridgeable gap
why-o why-o why-o   she can't crossover?

my mother is an indictment
i am fettered by the genes
directed before beginning
i cry **for** her
this is not capitulating blood
that run fast through my vein
i am the twice born
i take back her tail
to bury it in heartsoil
like placenta by tree and water it
i celebrate saving distance
embrace difference as identity as key
i cook yam say yes ma'am
i deeplisten to grayhairs
before memory flees
of Harlem as home
of being free...

my mother is an indictment
i cry for her
i take back her tail.

She knits acrylic hosannas
in lime green, pink and yellow
skeins of skinny spun dreams
dressing lamina dolls with painted
on shoes or only torsos topping
toilet paper with plantation-width
skirts. hooked loops from baby yarn
blue   yellow

Splay-legged as a boy on the train
gruff and sure with her hook
her needle flashing in dim
air flying fingers prowess
mammy-made woven-thread things
the weaver was a woman was a man

our dresser our clothier our maker
moves digits through small space
constriction shapes grace
Hope knew no halleluiahs
nothing in excelsis
her agnostic singer
ran riffs on necessity's inventions
mothering changes on blank fabrics
wringing the night's pause

whirring into dawn   whirring into dawn   whirring into dawn
easter ensembles winter protections
a style re:
visioned
whole,   sound.

My Mommy Gone #15

Every day another memory unveils its mystery

"You must be worried sick"

says radioman to poet on her teenager

at college.   I remember your

angry face in my dorm room

moments before your departure

when I mutter, "you'll be gone soon"

to your unwanted suggestions, questions

and now, lifetimes after your directions,

fire, and flash extinguished, I shiver,

realizing it was love's flame

when you burnt me.

To Every Birth Its Pain

No backporch in my mind
but there was beauty: sun
slowsetting on episcopal church
i thought it a cathedral, a castle
whose tropical tree peeked
from alley   from back
Gracing the gray sinful concrete
block with relief, recessed
between aging buildings.
Our playcries melted with fading day
carhorns, hustlenoise muted
like thin hornplayer's strain
for expression Strain for expression...
small store and efficient.
She peered between fronds
of her window jungle. (i would wonder:
was this like her home?)
calling me, softsmiling, smile worn
for me alone. Deep but small lap
soon outgrown, never outgrown
large bosom and salt and pepper
hair thickbraided, bound toward a knot.
Al/ways warm, comfort-fragrance
humming soothe lullabyes
"if i had the wings of a dove"
Ringing cash register,
giving cookies, talking silly,
girl little 'n banana brown
oh! the sugarcane mangoes
and bunbread oh! the caresshappiness
funnynames: *tutums*

Deep times. The nono African throat-
cluck, gently guiding, greatly indulging.
Growing fierce, steelfacedgranite

Strong: for the white bill creature
Cheated but never shortchanged

Old women Sundayscreeching in West Indian church
He arose! He arose! He Arose!

Defeated but victorious.

My tears still sting, water graveless places

starry airless spaces of dark and light

strung with long attenuated strings

memory's trembling filaments sing

their mourning songs, keening for beloveds

long gone sparks that shine but cannot ignite

across the void, the only comfort

in distant bright signal flares sputtering

incoherent insights. They're there, they're there

we're here

Hope in Paris

You let me take you far far away
where we beheld Grant and Hepburn smolder
and spark as they floated past glittering lights

Each night you giggled, whispering
endearments on the phone
recounting events to Daddy left at home

I had you all to myself
all to myself, all to myself
as it was in the beginning

When we watched movies in the black
blue dark, heaven of the warm Bronx
until dawn brought him back

And here you were shopping
for fabric on the Champs Elysées
thinned and tanned from all the seeing

to behold those long fragrant summer days
Saying 'allumettes' to light your tasty cigarettes
leaping in the air at La Défense, no *s'il vous plait*

That afternoon when I lost you
and went back to L'Opera's money exchange
checked with perfumers at Place Vendome

I was Orpheus without Eurydice
finally returning to the hotel
fearful of what the others would do to me

if I lost you. I prepared to hunt
but you were there, safe, waiting
smiling, *the Metro just another subway, baby*

you remembered the way without me
Not knowing as I wept and shouted
fumed and hugged you, that I was preparing

for a time soon to come

Recital

Afterward, each audience gathers to their star

My parents come close, my sister smiles, hugs me

My mother's large lamp eyes shine, each globe beams

My father harrumphs, we drift to the narrow hall

My teacher waits, leans forward for introductions

As others mill around the deconstructed ballroom

noises of relief, congratulations rise in happy frenzy

"Silk purse from sow's ears," father tells her. "Nonsense,"

teacher smiles, mother kisses me

We float slowly down wide, carpeted stairs

I clutch cool, curving banister for balance

Greensong rustles outside, ahead, doors flung wide

Birds celebrate late spring afternoon, sweet-sweet, calls

America is not at war with anyone, overtly

across Chemung River, Fall Brook manufactures television glass

Press Ware presses pyroceram dishes and pots

for tomorrow's kitchens. Hope heard arias

she sang to me as a child.

Worship

Herman Leonard exhibition, La Grande Halle,
Porte de la Villette, Paris 1990

The red mill is still
crowds fill the bandstand
and me, I felt overcome
kneeling before photos

the way they knelt in Notre Dame,
in Sacré-Coeur.
Images of my gone gods,
my patron saints

source of Mommy's hummed reveries
who peopled Daddy's tales
of fast life and past glories
always tainted, sainted by the near miss
or martyred by the kiss of caught up

all gone and what did I give them?
We shared some world, same time
To know the music, touch aural hems,
what did I want

alone in this rude foreign city?
I wanted to light a candle
before these pictures
I wanted to kneel.   I wanted to pray

to dark sparkling shoes
by china cup with the perfect lemon
his tea still shimmers hot
raiment shadow, ritual victual

these ghosts of a chance of a glory
that mine created   *holy holy holy*

O I kneel before Duke on stage,
shafts of light cleaving across
the black blank caressing his back,
a piano blooms before him

the feral face of Max
next to the melancholy round
of Brown, lost too soon,
young men sharp in their cool age

Billie's blouse had fabric-covered buttons
Sara leans, her sound a trajectory of grace
Ella's sweat, live rivulets...
what most remains through ubiquitous

smoke is their sound, that they played,
shaped life through air, that some
blind spark urged them on
to mount again the stage.

Resurrections

They are a happy couple, comfortable
in their knowledge of each other,
relaxed bodies, smiles, conversation
a gentle teasing of the detective
who still doesn't guess his wife's motives
or his daughter's but knows their hearts
better than any other and worries over all
between cases, strives to be good
for which they tease him when he fails

Makes me cry, as any good fiction
resurrects you, even the ones you wouldn't like
but would watch with mommy and tell me
you sussed it out before the end, you saw it
coming even as you sat still for our rough
ministrations as we braided your balding ring
examined your thick nails, pinched, poked
and tickled.   you made her endless
cups of tea that got cold, you confessed
that you weren't superman. i cast you in that role
anyway.   what returns is the love
when the stone rolls away
what flutters forth is love
why they wept not just for his tortures
but for the loss of his presence, scent of his sweat
his striving and kindness, his generosity, his huge heart,
blood warmth of his strong, large hand holding theirs
for the love they were left to carry
forth in the world, alone

About the Author

A third generation New Yorker, firstborn, Akua Lezli Hope has won two Artists Fellowships from the New York Foundation for the Arts, a Ragdale U.S.-Africa Fellowship, and a Creative Writing Fellowship from The National Endowment for The Arts. She's also won scholarships for the Hurston/Wright Foundation writing workshop and the Provincetown Fine Arts Work Center. She is a Cave Canem fellow, and has a B.A. in psychology from Williams College, a M.B.A. in marketing from Columbia University Graduate School of Business, and a M.S.J. in broadcast journalism from Columbia University Graduate School of Journalism.

Her first collection, *Embouchure, Poems on Jazz and Other Musics*, won the *Writer's Digest* book award for poetry. She is published in numerous literary magazines including *African American Review, Breath and Shadow, Catalyst, The Cossack Review, Eye to the Telescope, Hambone, Obsidian II, Stone Canoe*, and many others. Her work is included in anthologies including *The 100 Best African American Poems; The Crafty Poet II; The Year's Best Writing; Writer's Digest Guides; Dark Matter* (the first anthology of African American Science Fiction); *Will Work for Peace: New Political Poems; What Is Found There, Notebooks on Poetry and Politics* by Adrienne Rich (W.W. Norton); *Erotique Noir, an Anthology of Black Erotica* (Doubleday/Anchor); *Extended Outlooks;* and *The Iowa Review Collection of Contemporary Women Writers* among many others.

She is a founding member of the Black Writers Union and the New Renaissance Writers Guild. For a decade she led the Voices of Fire Reading Choir, performing her work and that of other African American poets. She also creates sculpture and adornments in fiber, glass, metal, and paper.

About the Artist

Globally renowned multi-media artist El Anatsui, born in 1944 in Anyanko, has been active for much of his career in Nigeria. He has received the Golden Lion for Lifetime Achievement, an honorary degree from Harvard University, and the Praemium Imperiale. His work has been shown in multitides of galleries and many major museums, including the Brooklyn Museum, the Clark Art Institute, the Metropolitan Museum of Art, the National Museum of African Art, the Smithsonian Institution, and many others.

About The Word Works

The Word Works, a nonprofit literary organization, publishes contemporary poetry and presents public programs. Imprints include The Washington Prize, International Editions, The Tenth Gate Prize, and the Hilary Tham Capital Collection. A reading period is also held in May.

Monthly, The Word Works offers free literary programs in the Chevy Chase, MD, Café Muse series, and each summer, it holds free poetry programs in Washington, D.C.'s Rock Creek Park. Annually in June, two high school students debut in the Joaquin Miller Poetry Series as winners of the Jacklyn Potter Young Poets Competition. Since 1974, Word Works programs have included: "In the Shadow of the Capitol," a symposium and archival project on the African American intellectual community in segregated Washington, D.C.; the Gunston Arts Center Poetry Series; the Poet Editor panel discussions at The Writer's Center; and Master Class workshops.

As a 501(c)3 organization, The Word Works has received awards from the National Endowment for the Arts, the National Endowment for the Humanities, the D.C. Commission on the Arts & Humanities, the Witter Bynner Foundation, Poets & Writers, The Writer's Center, Bell Atlantic, the David G. Taft Foundation, and others, including many generous private patrons.

The Word Works has established an archive of artistic and administrative materials in the Washington Writing Archive housed in the George Washington University Gelman Library. It is a member of the Council of Literary Magazines and Presses and its books are distributed by Small Press Distribution.

wordworksbooks.org

OTHER WORD WORKS BOOKS

Annik Adey-Babinski, *Okay Cool No Smoking Love Pony*
Karren L. Alenier, *Wandering on the Outside*
Karren L. Alenier, ed., *Whose Woods These Are*
Karren L. Alenier & Miles David Moore, eds., *Winners: A Retrospective of the Washington Prize*
Christopher Bursk, ed., *Cool Fire*
Willa Carroll, *Nerve Chorus*
Grace Cavalieri, *Creature Comforts*
Barbara Goldberg, *Berta Broadfoot and Pepin the Short*
Frannie Lindsay, *If Mercy*
Elaine Maggarrell, *The Madness of Chefs*
Marilyn McCabe, *Glass Factory*
JoAnne McFarland, *Identifying the Body*
Kevin McLellan, *Ornitheology*
Leslie McGrath, *Feminists Are Passing from Our Lives*
Ann Pelletier, *Letter That Never*
Ayaz Pirani, *Happy You Are Here*
W.T. Pfefferle, *My Coolest Shirt*
Jacklyn Potter, Dwaine Rieves, Gary Stein, eds., *Cabin Fever: Poets at Joaquin Miller's Cabin*
Robert Sargent, *Aspects of a Southern Story & A Woman from Memphis*
Miles Waggener, *Superstition Freeway*
Fritz Ward, *Tsunami Diorama*
Amber West, *Hen & God*
Nancy White, ed., *Word for Word*

INTERNATIONAL EDITIONS

Kajal Ahmad (Alana Marie Levinson-LaBrosse, Mewan Nahro Said Sofi and Darya Abdul-Karim Ali Najin, trans., with Barbara Goldberg), *Handful of Salt*
Keyne Cheshire (trans.), *Murder at Jagged Rock: A Tragedy by Sophocles*
Jeanette L. Clariond (Curtis Bauer, trans.), *Image of Absence*
Jean Cocteau (Mary-Sherman Willis, trans.), *Grace Notes*
Yoko Danno & James C. Hopkins, *The Blue Door*
Moshe Dor, Barbara Goldberg, Giora Leshem, eds., *The Stones Remember: Native Israeli Poets*
Moshe Dor (Barbara Goldberg, trans.), *Scorched by the Sun*
Lee Sang (Myong-Hee Kim, trans.), *Crow's Eye View: The Infamy of Lee Sang, Korean Poet*
Vladimir Levchev (Henry Taylor, trans.), *Black Book of the Endangered Species*

THE TENTH GATE PRIZE
Jennifer Barber, *Works on Paper*, 2015
Lisa Lewis, *Taxonomy of the Missing*, 2017
Roger Sedarat, *Haji As Puppet*, 2016
Lisa Sewell, *Impossible Object*, 2014

THE WASHINGTON PRIZE
Nathalie Anderson, *Following Fred Astaire*, 1998
Michael Atkinson, *One Hundred Children Waiting for a Train*, 2001
Molly Bashaw, *The Whole Field Still Moving Inside It*, 2013
Carrie Bennett, *biography of water*, 2004
Peter Blair, *Last Heat*, 1999
John Bradley, *Love-in-Idleness: The Poetry of Roberto Zingarello*,
    1995, 2ND edition 2014
Christopher Bursk, *The Way Water Rubs Stone*, 1988
Richard Carr, *Ace*, 2008
Jamison Crabtree, *Rel[AM]ent*, 2014
Jessica Cuello, *Hunt*, 2016
Barbara Duffey, *Simple Machines*, 2015
B. K. Fischer, *St. Rage's Vault*, 2012
Linda Lee Harper, *Toward Desire*, 1995
Ann Rae Jonas, *A Diamond Is Hard But Not Tough*, 1997
Susan Lewis, *Zoom*, 2017
Frannie Lindsay, *Mayweed*, 2009
Richard Lyons, *Fleur Carnivore*, 2005
Elaine Magarrell, *Blameless Lives*, 1991
Fred Marchant, *Tipping Point*, 1993, 2ND edition 2013
Ron Mohring, *Survivable World*, 2003
Barbara Moore, *Farewell to the Body*, 1990
Brad Richard, *Motion Studies*, 2010
Jay Rogoff, *The Cutoff*, 1994
Prartho Sereno, *Call from Paris*, 2007, 2ND edition 2013
Enid Shomer, *Stalking the Florida Panther*, 1987
John Surowiecki, *The Hat City After Men Stopped Wearing Hats*, 2006
Miles Waggener, *Phoenix Suites*, 2002
Charlotte Warren, *Gandhi's Lap*, 2000
Mike White, *How to Make a Bird with Two Hands*, 2011
Nancy White, *Sun, Moon, Salt*, 1992, 2ND edition 2010
George Young, *Spinoza's Mouse*, 1996

THE HILARY THAM CAPITAL COLLECTION

Nathalie Anderson, *Stain*
Mel Belin, *Flesh That Was Chrysalis*
Carrie Bennett, *The Land Is a Painted Thing*
Doris Brody, *Judging the Distance*
Sarah Browning, *Whiskey in the Garden of Eden*
Grace Cavalieri, *Pinecrest Rest Haven*
Cheryl Clarke, *By My Precise Haircut*
Christopher Conlon, *Gilbert and Garbo in Love*
       & *Mary Falls: Requiem for Mrs. Surratt*
Donna Denizé, *Broken like Job*
W. Perry Epes, *Nothing Happened*
David Eye, *Seed*
Bernadette Geyer, *The Scabbard of Her Throat*
Barbara G. S. Hagerty, *Twinzilla*
James Hopkins, *Eight Pale Women*
Donald Illich, *Chance Bodies*
Brandon Johnson, *Love's Skin*
Thomas March, *Aftermath*
Marilyn McCabe, *Perpetual Motion*
Judith McCombs, *The Habit of Fire*
James McEwen, *Snake Country*
Miles David Moore, *The Bears of Paris*
       & *Rollercoaster*
Kathi Morrison-Taylor, *By the Nest*
Tera Vale Ragan, *Reading the Ground*
Michael Shaffner, *The Good Opinion of Squirrels*
Maria Terrone, *The Bodies We Were Loaned*
Hilary Tham, *Bad Names for Women*
       & *Counting*
Barbara Ungar, *Charlotte Brontë, You Ruined My Life*
       & *Immortal Medusa*
Jonathan Vaile, *Blue Cowboy*
Rosemary Winslow, *Green Bodies*
Michele Wolf, *Immersion*
Joe Zealberg, *Covalence*

www.ingramcontent.com/pod-product-compliance
Lightning Source LLC
Chambersburg PA
CBHW031000090426
42737CB00008B/620